FLAGS of the United States

Mark Lloyd

GALLERY BOOKS

An imprint of W. H. Smith Publishers Inc.
112 Madison Avenue
New York, New York 10016

INTRODUCTION

The United States of America is probably unique among nations in depicting its historical growth through the changes in the design of the national flag, which shows accurately, at specific dates, the growing number of states in the Union.

In 1776 the American flag was adopted which consisted of 13 red and white stripes with the British Union Jack in the canton, each stripe representing one of the 13 colonies. In 1777 Congress adopted a flag of alternate red and white stripes with 13 white stars on a blue field. Then, in 1794, when Vermont and Kentucky were admitted, there were 15 stars and 15 stripes (the flag becoming known as the "Star Spangled Banner"), but in 1818 the decision was made to revert to the 13 stripes as emblems of the original 13 states but to show 20 stars for the then number of states. Thereafter, each time a state was added to the Union a new star was added to the flag. The most recent to be added was that of Hawaii on 4 July 1960.

The consciousness of Americans of the importance of "Old Glory" indicates a strong love of their flag, a love which is also apparent in the enthusiasm they have for state flags. In these, all 50 of which are represented in this volume, the reader will find a great variety of pictorial content, much of it depicting the homely virtues of the labor so crucial to the creation and subsequent growth of the nation.

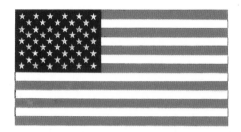

UNITED STATES OF AMERICA

Capital	Washington D.C.
Population	238,700,000
Area	3,539,289 sq miles
Largest Cities	New York, Chicago, Los Angeles, Philadelphia
National Motto	In God we trust
National Anthem	*The Star-Spangled Banner*

DISTRICT OF COLUMBIA

While not a state, the District of Columbia, a federal district of 69 square miles, was designated for Washington, the capital, and it too has its own flag. This is the banner of the arms of George Washington's family, who lived at Sulgrave Manor, a beautiful country house in Northamptonshire, England.

ALABAMA

The Cotton State

The flag of Alabama, like some of the flags mentioned later, is a reminder of the Confederate Battle Flag used during the Civil War.

In 1903 some members of the United Confederate Veterans expressed concern that the Battle Flag was subject to "incorrect representations in historical works" and asked their Headquarters to "ascertain all acceptable data." On 3 June 1906, Stephen D. Lee, General Commanding the Veterans, directed that the Battle Flag be "square, having a Greek Cross (saltire) of blue, edged with white, with thirteen equal white five-pointed stars; upon a red field; the whole bordered with white." The Infantry flag was 48 inches square, the blue arms of the cross 7½ inches wide, the white edging to the cross ½ inch wide and the white border around the flag 1½ inches wide. The stars were to be within a circle of 6-inch diameter. The Artillery flag was 36 inches square and the Cavalry flag 30 inches square, with all other measurements reduced in proportion.

The current flag of Alabama is a crimson cross on a white field and was adopted in 1895. Although square, the dimensions are not laid down by law.

The state governor's flag is similar, but carries the state seal in the top triangle and the state crest in the lower one. The crest shows a boll of cotton, one of Alabama's major products.

History	First settled by the French when part of Louisiana but ceded to Britain in 1763; in 1802 became part of Mississippi Territory. A territory in its own right in 1817, admitted to the Union on 14 December 1819. Seceded on 11 January 1861 and re-admitted in 1868
Area	51,998 sq miles
Population	3,893,888
Capital	Montgomery
Largest City	Birmingham
Major Products	Steel, chemicals, textiles, coal, cement, stone, petroleum, cotton, poultry, cattle
State Motto	We dare defend our rights
State Colors	Red and white
Bird	Yellowhammer
Tree	Southern Pine
Flower	Camellia

ALASKA

The Great Land ◆ The Last Frontier

Discovered in 1741 by Bering, Alaska lies at the northwestern extremity of the U.S.A. A competition to design a flag was won in 1927 by Benny Benson, a 13-year-old who received $1,000 for his efforts. His winning design was made official by the territorial legislature on 2 May of that year.

Alaska's northerly position was obviously Benny Benson's inspiration for his design, which shows the large North Star with the Great Bear below it.

When Alaska was given statehood in 1959 the flag remained the same. The legislation of 1927 had specified the dimensions of the flag and decreed that the stars were to be the yellow colour of natural gold, on a field of the same blue as appears on the Stars and Stripes. This was the only alteration to Benny Benson's original design, which had used a forget-me-not blue to match the state flower.

The width of the flag to the length is in the proportion of 125:177. The diameter of the North Star is one-tenth of the width and the stars of the Great Bear are three-fifths the diameter of the North Star.

The state seal, dating from 1910, also depicts the Northern Lights but the Great Bear does not appear.

History	Alaska lies in the extreme north-west of the American continent, facing Siberia. Settled by Russian traders from 1744 and run by the Russian-American Company, which sold it to the U.S.A. in 1867 for $7.2 million. From 1884 it was a district of Oregon; became a Territory in 1913, and admitted to the Union on 3 January 1959
Area	586,412 sq miles (the largest state)
Population	401,851
Capital	Juneau
Largest City	Anchorage
Major Products	Oil, minerals, timber, fish
State Motto	North to the future
Bird	Ptarmigan
Tree	Sitka Spruce
Flower	Forget-me-not

ARIZONA

The Grand Canyon State

The history of Arizona is closely linked to that of Spain and goes back to 1539, when it was first visited by a Spanish Franciscan monk, Marcos de Niza. In 1824 it became part of the United Mexican States, and passed to the U.S.A. in 1848 after the Mexican War. The name is believed to derive from the Spanish *arida-zona* (dry belt).

Arizona did not have a flag until 1911, when one was designed for a rifle team from the Territory which had entered a competition in Ohio. The Territory's Adjutant-General, Charles Harris, quickly designed a flag for the occasion. Arizona was admitted to the Union in 1912 and the flag was made official in 1917.

The deserts of Arizona are extremely arid and have the highest temperatures in the U.S.A. Harris indicated that his design was meant to show the sun setting over the desert while the colors recalled the many years of Spanish domination. The central star is copper-colored, symbolizing the main mineral found in the state, and the blue lower half represented the United States.

Before the flag was officially adopted in 1917 there were many other suggestions put forward but Harris's design eventually prevailed, with a few small changes.

The state seal, containing the motto *Ditat Deus*, is worked into the floor of the state Capitol. The representation is an impressive 15 feet in diameter.

History	In the south-west of the U.S.A. between the Colorado River and Mexico, and contains the Grand Canyon. First settled in 1752, when part of Mexico. Part of the huge territory ceded by Mexico to the U.S.A. in 1848. Became a Territory in 1863; admitted to the Union on 14 February 1912
Area	113,508 sq miles
Population	3,296,000
Capital	Phoenix
Largest City	Phoenix
Major Products	Cotton, livestock, cereals, minerals (especially copper)
State Motto	*Ditat Deus* ("God enriches")
Bird	Cactus Wren
Tree	Paloverde
Flower	Saguaro cactus blossom

ARKANSAS

The Land of Opportunity

The flag of Arkansas is another reminder of the Confederate Battle Flag with its blue diagonals and white stars. The powerful Daughters of the American Revolution put pressure on the authorities to adopt an official flag for presentation to the battleship *Arkansas* and the original design was drawn up by one of the Daughters, Miss Willie Hocker.

Arkansas was one of three states formed from the Louisiana Purchase of 1803, when the U.S.A. bought the territory from France. Miss Hocker indicated that the three blue stars in the center of the flag were meant to represent those three states. The 25 white stars are a reminder that Arkansas was the twenty-fifth state to be admitted to the Union. The red, white and blue colors represent both the Confederacy and the tricolor of France.

The original design had only the three stars in the center but the name of the state was added at the flag's official adoption in February 1913 and the upper blue star first appeared in 1924. It represents the Confederacy.

Although the U.S.A. is rich in minerals, Arkansas is the only state to have diamonds, hence the diamond shape on the red field. Further acknowledgment of the uniqueness of the diamond came in 1967 when it was officially declared the state gem. Arkansas is also called The Wonder State because of its remarkable natural features.

History	On river of same name, and west of the Mississippi. Was part of Louisiana territory sold to the U.S.A. in 1803 for $15 million. Area first settled in 1686; with rest of Louisiana belonged to Spain 1763-1800. Became a Territory in 1819; admitted to the Union on 15 June 1836. Seceded on 6 May 1861, and re-admitted on 22 June 1868
Area	53,187 sq miles
Population	2,286,435
Capital	Little Rock
Largest City	Little Rock
Major Products	Bauxite and other minerals, rice, poultry, cotton, manufactured goods
State Motto	*Regnat populus* ("The people rule")
Bird	Mocking Bird (1929)
Tree	Pine (1939)
Flower	Apple blossom (1901)

CALIFORNIA

The Golden State

CALIFORNIA REPUBLIC

A flag with a red star was hoisted in 1836 by Californian settlers who wanted independence from Mexico. Ten years later the red star reappeared, together with the components of today's flag, when a further attempt was made to form an independent state. The grizzly bear, although the official animal of California, is now extinct but in 1846 would have been ideal as a symbol of ferocity. The devastating earthquake of 1906 in San Francisco saw the loss of the original design of the flag and the state was without one until 1911. Legislation in that year produced today's flag which is meant to be a recreation of the original.

The grizzly bear also appears on the state seal, first adopted in 1849. The state governor's flag dates from 1957 and consists of a blue field with a white star in each corner and the state seal in the center.

The state colors are blue and gold, the latter representing the discovery of gold in 1848 and the gold rush of '49. Although mining continues on a large scale, petroleum has now outstripped gold in importance to the state economy.

History	Part of the Spanish and Mexican territories. Before the war with Mexico settlers declared an independent state at Sonoma, and raised the American flag at Monterey. Became a state on 9 September 1850
Area	158,693 sq miles
Population	23,667,902
Capital	Sacramento
Largest City	Los Angeles
Major Products	Oil, natural gas, minerals, gold, cotton, fruit, livestock, timber, fish, manufactured goods, aerospace, electronics, tourism
State Motto	I have found it (*Eureka*)
State Colors	Blue and gold
Animal	Grizzly Bear (1953)
Bird	California Valley Quail (1931)
Tree	California Redwood (1931)
Flower	Golden Poppy (1903)

COLORADO

The Centennial State ◆ The Columbine State

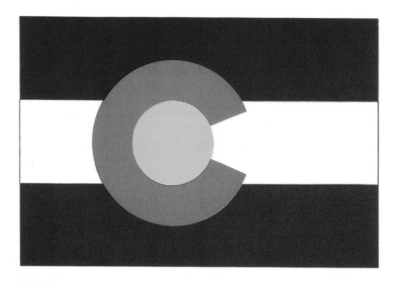

Although the flag of Colorado was originally meant by its designer, Andrew Carlisle Carson, to be as we see it here, its official specifications were mysteriously altered upon its adoption in 1911. The legislation specified that the red C with the yellow center should be much smaller and placed immediately next to the flagstaff. In practice the flag was made as it is seen today and was eventually made "legal" in March 1964. Carson had also specified that the blue field should be the same color as the columbine, the state flower, but in 1929 this was officially changed to the blue of Old Glory.

Entering the Union in 1876, Colorado is known as the Centennial State or the Columbine State and the red C can stand for either of these or for the name of the state itself. Colorado was for many years ruled by Spain, the name meaning "red" in Spanish. Like Arizona, the red and yellow also recall the Spanish colors. The Rocky Mountain Columbine is blue, white and gold, so that these colors are cleverly reflected in the flag. The gold also recalls the founding of Denver following the gold rush of 1858.

The mining of coal, silver and lead later became important industries and these are reflected in the state seal which has a shield depicting the Rocky Mountains and a selection of miners' tools. Until Carson's design of 1911, this shield appeared on the first flag in the center of a blue field.

History	Was partly in French Louisiana and partly in Spanish (later Mexican) territory. The French part passed to the U.S.A. in 1803 and the Mexican in 1848. Became a Territory in 1861; admitted to the Union on 1 August 1876
Area	104,090 sq miles
Population	2,889,964
Capital	Denver
Largest City	Denver
Major Products	Oil, gas, minerals, maize, wheat, potatoes, manufactured goods. Major tourist center; 20 million visits a year
State Motto	*Nil sine numine* ("Nothing without the Deity")
Bird	Lark Bunting
Tree	Blue Spruce
Flower	Rocky Mountain Columbine

CONNECTICUT

The Nutmeg State

Connecticut was settled in 1634 by Puritan colonists from Massachusetts and in 1639 adopted the famous Fundamental Orders which in many respects foreshadowed the United States Constitution. The state emblem dates from around 1647 and consisted of a seal showing grapevines and the motto *Transtulit qui sustinet*. The seal of 1711 had only three vines, perhaps meant to represent the colonies of Connecticut, Saybrook and New Haven.

During the Revolutionary War against the British in 1775 the Connecticut troops used this seal on their flag, which is among the most ancient of American flags. The words of the motto were changed around in the seal which was adopted in 1931 and is in use today. It is surrounded by an oval band which has the words "Seal of the Republic of Connecticut" in Latin.

A nineteenth-century flag consisting of a blue field with the arms in the center was officially adopted in 1895 after pressure from the doughty Daughters of the American Revolution. Regulations of 3 June 1897 specified that the arms should be in color in the center of a field of azure blue. Although the dimensions were to be "squarish," further regulations in 1957 meant that the flag is in fact usually in the proportions of 2:3.

The colony received its first Charter in 1662 and the state tree, the white oak, commemorates the hiding of the Charter in the Charter Tree at Hartford, Connecticut.

History	First settled in 1634; adopted its first constitution five years later. Took over Saybrook in 1644 and New Haven in 1662, when the colony received its first Charter. Became a republican state in 1776 and ratified the U.S. constitution in 1788
Area	5,018 sq miles (third smallest state)
Population	3,107,576
Capital	Hartford
Largest City	Bridgeport
Major Products	Manufactured goods (machinery, transportation equipment), dairy products, livestock, silage
State Motto	*Qui transtulit sustinet* ("He who transplanted sustains")
Bird	Robin (1943)
Tree	White Oak
Flower	Mountain Laurel (1907)

DELAWARE

The First State ◆ The Diamond State

Like Connecticut, Delaware was one of the original thirteen states of the U.S.A. and is named after Lord de la Warr, Governor of Virginia 1610-1618. The state is generally agricultural and this is reflected in the coat of arms which dates from 1777. A soldier and a farmer support a shield depicting a wheatsheaf, an ear of corn and an ox. Delaware is also a maritime state and this is represented by the crest of a ship in full sail. The arms were used on flags carried by Delaware troops during the Civil War, but without the diamond shape which was only added after the flag was officially adopted in July 1913. The colors of blue and colonial buff recall the colors of the uniform worn during the Revolution and the diamond echoes Delaware's nickname – The Diamond State. The date toward the bottom of the blue field reminds us that Delaware was the first state to ratify the U.S. Constitution.

The flag of the state governor is similar to the flag in current use but has a gold fringe. The state bird is a fighting cock and this also appears on the governor's flag in the form of a finial to the flagstaff.

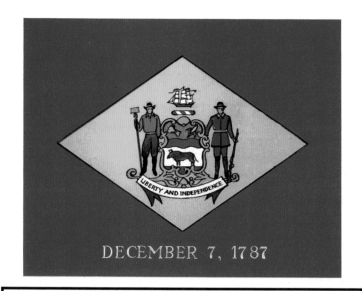

DECEMBER 7, 1787

History	First settled by Dutch in 1631, then by Swedes who named it "New Sweden" (1638-55). In 1674 it passed to Britain. Was a dependency of Pennsylvania until 1776, then became a separate state. First state to ratify U.S. Constitution, on 7 December 1787
Area	2,044 sq miles (second smallest state)
Population	594,338
Capital	Dover
Largest City	Wilmington
Major Products	Chemicals, transport equipment, processed food, livestock, corn, soybeans
State Motto	Liberty and independence
Bird	Blue Hen Fighting Cock
Tree	American Holly
Flower	Peach blossom

FLORIDA

The Sunshine State

Florida is named after the day of its discovery in 1513 by a Spaniard. It was Easter Day, which in Spanish is *pascua florida*.

Florida was admitted to the Union in 1845 but seceded in 1861, at which time it created a new state seal. This showed the Florida swamps with an Indian woman in the foreground and a steamboat sailing past a setting sun. After the Civil War this seal was used on the state's new flag, appearing in the center of a plain white field. The red cross of St. Andrew (the saltire) was added in 1900, five years after it was used by Alabama, and was probably taken from the Battle Flag of the Confederacy. Although there is no documentary evidence to support this, it does seem more than coincidence.

Before being admitted to the Union in 1845, Florida had been ruled over by both the Spanish and the British and therefore had had a number of flags. After 1845 a flag was created for the new state, consisting of five bands of blue, orange, red, white and green together with the Stars and Stripes in the upper quarter and the motto "Leave us alone" within a scroll. This flag was never used, however, and after leaving the Union in 1861 the Florida troops adopted a version of the Stars and Stripes which had only one large white star. On re-admission to the Union in 1868 the state used the plain white flag with the seal until the current flag was ratified in 1900.

History	First permanent settlement at St. Augustine on 8 September 1565. Except for 1763-83, Florida belonged to Spain until 1821, when ceded to the U.S.A. Was a Territory until 3 March 1845, when admitted to the Union. Seceded in 1861; re-admitted in 1868
Area	58,664 sq miles
Population	9,746,324
Capital	Tallahassee
Largest City	Jacksonville
Major Products	Citrus fruits, melons, vegetables, soy-beans, sugar-cane, tobacco, fish, sea-food, metalware, timber, processed food. Tourism: 35 million tourists annually
State Motto	In God we trust
Bird	Mocking Bird (1927)
Tree	Sabal Palm (1953)
Flower	Orange blossom (1909)

GEORGIA

The Empire State of the South

Georgia was founded by the British in 1733 and named after King George II. After the Revolutionary War it became a state in 1776, seceded from the Union in 1861 and was re-admitted in July 1870.

Georgia is another state whose flag recalls the Confederacy, having used a version of the Stars and Bars during the Civil War. The Stars and Bars was the first Confederate flag and was recommended by the "Committee on a Proper Flag for the Confederate States of America" in its report of 4 March 1861. The Committee laid down that the flag should be "of a red field with a white space extending horizontally through the center and equal in width to one-third of the flag, the red spaces above and below to be of the same width as the white. The union blue extending down through the white space and stopping at the lower red space. In the center of the union a circle of white stars corresponding in number (seven) with the States in the Confederacy." Georgian troops used this flag during the Civil War with the state seal within the seven stars.

In 1879 the new state flag was similar but with the blue canton extended to the full depth of the flag and without the seal or the stars. The seal was restored in 1905 and in 1914 was slightly changed to show the date of 1776.

The present flag came into being on 1 July 1956, the bars of the old Stars and Bars flag being replaced by the Confederate Battle Flag.

History	Georgia lies south of Savannah River and north of Florida with an Atlantic sea-coast. Received a Charter in 1732, made a royal province in 1752. Became a state in 1776; ratified the Constitution on 2 January 1788; seceded on 19 January 1861; re-admitted on 15 July 1870
Area	58,910 sq miles
Population	5,463,105
Capital	Atlanta
Largest City	Atlanta
Major Products	Cotton, corn, wheat, soybeans, textiles, kaolin, wood products and paper
State Motto	Wisdom, justice and moderation
State Colors	Red, white and blue
Bird	Brown Thrasher (1935)
Tree	Live Oak (1937)
Flower	Cherokee Rose (1916)

HAWAII

The Aloha State

When Captain Cook first landed in Hawaii in 1778, one of his companions was George Vancouver who revisited the islands in 1793 and presented the King with a Union Jack. Until 1816 Hawaii was under British protection and took as its flag the Union Jack which today still makes up a part of the flag of the 50th state of the U.S.A.

In 1816, with the British having gone, the King kept the Union Jack in the canton of his new flag with the rest of the flag made up of varying numbers of red, white and blue stripes. The number of stripes became eight in 1845, each stripe representing one of the main islands in the Hawaiian chain.

This flag has remained constant during many changes in Hawaii's history, including the take-over by American settlers in 1893, the establishment of a Republic in 1894, annexation as a Territory in 1898 and admission to the Union in 1959.

In 1896 the Republic adopted a seal and a coat of arms, both of which are the basis of the present ones. The 1896 versions were adapted from the King's arms of the 1850s, but in the modern version the royal crown has been replaced by a symbol of the rising sun and the religious devices have been removed in favor of a central star.

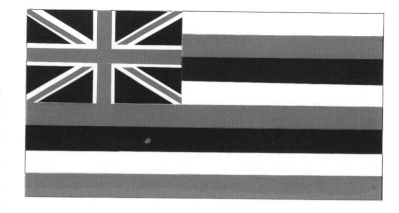

History	Pacific islands, originally inhabited only by Polynesians. First visited by Captain Cook in 1778. U.S. settlers deposed ruling Queen in 1893 and formed an independent republic. Annexed to the U.S.A. in 1898 as a Territory; admitted to the Union in 1959
Area	6,471 sq miles including 136 islands (7 inhabited)
Population	964,961 (12.3% Hawaiians)
Capital	Honolulu
Largest City	Honolulu
Major Products	Sugar, pineapples. Tourism: about 7 million visits per year
State Motto	The life of the land is perpetuated by righteousness
Bird	*Nene* (Hawaiian goose)
Tree	*Kukui*
Flower	Hibiscus

IDAHO

The Gem State

When Idaho was given statehood in 1890, some aspects of its old Territorial seal were incorporated into the new state seal, designed in 1891 by Miss Emma Edwards. The coat of arms was supported on one side by the female figure of Liberty and Justice and on the other by a miner carrying a pickaxe and shovel. Within the shield was a landscape including the emblematic state tree, the Western White Pine. Surrounding the shield were two horns of plenty, a wheatsheaf, some rocks and vegetation. The crest was an elk's head with the state motto within a scroll. The one star at the foot of the surrounding rim indicated that Idaho was a new state.

The first flag of 1907 simply called for the name of the state to appear on a field of blue, but invariably the seal also appeared, usually in full color and with a gold surround. The name appears on a red scroll beneath the seal.

The flag was authorized by legislation in March 1927 and thirty years later Miss Edwards' surviving original artwork was brought into use for both the official seal and the flag.

Although lumbering, agriculture and livestock-raising are the principal industries, Emma Edwards' depiction of a miner was also appropriate as minerals in the state include lead, zinc, silver, gold and copper.

History	Idaho lies in the north-west; was once part of the Oregon Country shared between the U.S.A. and Britain (1818-48). Following the 1860 gold strike settlers and miners arrived and Idaho became a Territory in 1863. Admitted to the Union on 3 July 1890
Area	83,564 sq miles
Population	943,935
Capital	Boise
Largest City	Boise
Major Products	Potatoes, wheat, timber, minerals, including silver
State Motto	*Esto perpetua* ("May it endure forever")
Bird	Mountain Bluebird (1931)
Tree	Western White Pine
Flower	Syringa (1931)

ILLINOIS

The Prairie State

When Illinois was still only a Territory its seal was already showing the American eagle. That version was a straight-forward rendering of the eagle with a shield, as in the emblem of the United States, and the current rendering first appeared when Illinois was admitted to the Union in December 1818. In its beak the eagle holds a flying red scroll bearing the state motto and stands on a rock against which is leaning a shield containing the Stars and Stripes. Behind the shield is a laurel wreath and on the rocks are the dates 1818 and 1868, the latter being the date of a recutting of the seal. At that time there was a suggestion that the two phrases of the state motto should be reversed. This was defeated, but the person cutting the seal very cleverly arranged the scroll so that the last two words of the motto are read first, thereby achieving the object.

The Daughters of the American Revolution were yet again instrumental in organizing a competition for the design of a state flag, in 1915. The winning design came from some of their members in Rockford, Illinois, and was given to the state legislature. The name of the state was added to the flag in July 1970, beneath a fuller colored version of the state seal.

ILLINOIS

History	Illinois is really a Mississippi valley state which also borders on Lake Michigan. First explored by the French in 1673 and belonged to French Louisiana. Part of the Indiana Territory ceded by France to Britain in 1763; conceded by Britain to the U.S.A. in 1783. Became a Territory in 1809; admitted to the Union on 3 December 1818
Area	56,400 sq miles
Population	11,426,518
Capital	Springfield
Largest City	Chicago
Major Products	Manufactured goods, food products, coal, livestock, maize, soybeans
State Motto	State sovereignty – national union
Bird	Eastern Cardinal
Tree	Oak
Flower	Meadow Violet

INDIANA

The Hoosier State

The state of Indiana officially has two flags, although only the second is commonly used. This came about because until 1901 there was no state flag and it was decided to adopt the Stars and Stripes to serve the purpose. In 1916, the centenary of the state, the Daughters of the American Revolution ran a competition for the design of a state flag and the current design by Paul Hadley was chosen as winner. His design was officially approved by the state legislature in May 1917 and was adopted by law in 1955 – but the law of 1901 adopting the Stars and Stripes was never repealed and therefore leaves the state with two official flags.

Hadley's design shows the torch of Liberty surrounded by an outer ring of 13 stars representing the original states with an inner ring of five stars to represent the next five states admitted to the Union. Above the flame of the torch is a larger single star representing Indiana, with the name of the state placed above it. The whole is in gold on a blue field.

The state seal is extremely complex and has hardly been altered since its inception in 1801, a year after Indiana became a Territory.

History	Similar in many ways to Illinois, and also first explored by the French. Settlements made in 1732-33; ceded to Britain in 1763 as the Indiana Territory. Became a Territory in its own right in 1800; admitted to the Union on 11 December 1816
Area	36,185 sq miles
Population	5,490,224
Capital	Indianapolis
Largest City	Indianapolis
Major Products	Maize, wheat, oats, soybeans, coal, oil, manufactured goods
State Motto	The Crossroads of America (1937)
Bird	Cardinal (1933)
Tree	Tulip Tree (1931)
Flower	Peony (1957)

IOWA

The Hawkeye State

The seal of Iowa dates from 1847, the year after the state was admitted to the Union. The seal depicts a soldier holding a flag with the Cap of Liberty, together with a flying eagle holding a scroll in its beak. It is this eagle which was taken from the seal and used on the flag.

In 1917, American soldiers in France were sent copies of their state flags by their families, except those soldiers from states such as Iowa, which had no flag. Again it was the Daughters of the American Revolution who set out to remedy this omission. The eagle and scroll were taken from the state seal and put onto a white field, together with the name of the state.

Many people were unhappy about this and felt that state flags were unnecessary when one flag, the Stars and Stripes, could serve as an expression of national unity. It therefore took until March 1921 for the present flag to be adopted by the state legislature.

A member of the Daughters suggested that Iowa's part in the Louisiana Purchase of 1803 should be indicated by the addition of the French red, white and blue, and this idea was officially adopted.

History	Lies across the Mississippi from Illinois; until 1803 part of French Louisiana. First settled in 1788; became a Territory in 1838, the third from the Louisiana Purchase. Admitted to the Union on 28 December 1846
Area	56,275 sq miles
Population	2,913,808
Capital	Des Moines
Largest City	Des Moines
Major Products	Corn, soybeans, livestock (especially pig-meat), coal, manufactured goods
State Motto	Our liberties we prize and our rights we will maintain
Bird	Eastern Goldfinch
Tree	Oak
Flower	Wild Rose

KANSAS

The Sunflower State

Many state seals show idealized allegorical landscapes, and none more so than Kansas. It is the principal winter wheat-producing area and the seal shows a ploughman in the foreground preparing his field for sowing. The rising sun appears in the background and in the sky there are 34 stars, symbolic of the states which were in the Union in 1861, the date of the seal.

The native wild sunflower from which the state takes its nickname was adopted as the state flower in 1903. A flag was produced in 1925 which consisted of a blue field containing the sunflower and the state seal in the center. However, the seal was so large that it overwhelmed the flower and in March 1927 the design was altered and adopted as the official state flag. The revised version had a smaller version of the seal with the sunflower above it, resting on a twisted wreath of blue and gold. The name of the state was added on 30 June 1963, to make the flag more easily identifiable.

A second flag, a blue field with a large single sunflower, was officially adopted on 30 June 1953 as the state banner for use in parades by the National Guard. Individual National Guardsmen use the same design on their uniforms as a shoulder flash.

History	Originally part of French Louisiana; settlement began about 1727. In 1763 ceded to Spain; in 1800 back to France; in 1803 to the U.S.A. as part of Louisiana Purchase. Became a Territory in 1854 and a state of the Union on 29 January 1861
Area	82,277 sq miles
Population	2,363,679
Capital	Topeka
Largest City	Wichita
Major Products	Wheat, maize, sorghum, livestock, coal, oil, gas, processed food, gasoline, aircraft
State Motto	*Ad astra per aspera* ("To the stars through difficulties")
Animal	American Buffalo (1955)
Bird	Western Meadowlark (1937)
Tree	Cottonwood (1937)
Flower	Sunflower (1903)

KENTUCKY

The Bluegrass State

Kentucky achieved statehood a few years after the original thirteen and its seal of 1792 shows what were described as "two friends embracing." They were accompanied by the state motto and name. The early version showed the two men standing on the edge of a cliff and dressed as frontiersmen, but nowadays, the precipice has gone and the dress is more modern – although not by much.

Like other Union states during the Civil War, Kentucky had a blue flag with its seal in the center and in 1880 this was made the official flag of the National Guard. In March 1918 the state legislature decided to adopt a new flag, but it was not until ten years later that a design was made. A simplified version of the state seal appears in the center of a blue field. The name of the state appears in condensed gold lettering in an arc around the top half of the seal and two sprigs of the state flower, goldenrod, form another arc around the lower half. This was declared official in later legislation of June 1962.

In 1926 the Kentucky Cardinal was named as the state bird. The 1962 legislation specified a finial for the flagstaff, which is a Cardinal in a pose described as "alert but restful."

History	Kentucky lies west across the Appalachians from Virginia. First settled from there in 1765 and was in effect a colony of Virginia until it achieved statehood in its own right on 1 June 1792 (the second to do so after the original 13)
Area	40,409 sq miles
Population	3,660,777
Capital	Frankfort
Largest City	Louisville
Major Products	Coal, oil, gas, tobacco, corn, livestock, machinery, tourism
State Motto	United we stand, divided we fall
Animal	Grey Squirrel (1968)
Bird	Kentucky Cardinal (1926)
Tree	Kentucky Coffee Tree (1976)
Flower	Goldenrod (1926)

LOUISIANA

The Pelican State

The Louisiana pelican made its first appearance on the state seal when statehood was achieved in 1812, but nothing is known beyond this as the original seal has long since disappeared. When the state seceded from the Union in 1861 the pelican made a reappearance on the state flag, but this too has not been seen since being captured by Admiral David Farragut during his defeat of the Confederate fleet in 1862. An earlier state flag, dating from 1851, consisted of blue, white and red stripes with a yellow star within a blue canton. This survived as the state flag right up to the end of the Civil War. Louisiana had rival governors in 1864, with the Federal governor using the word "Union" in his seal and the Confederate one employing the word "Justice," both words being taken from the state motto.

A new state seal was created in 1902, but in place of a natural pelican it was decided to depict an heraldic one. In European heraldry the pelican is invariably shown pecking at its own breast in order to feed its young and indicates piety and self-sacrifice. In the Louisiana version the pelican is feeding three of its chicks in the nest. The state motto is on a scroll which arcs to follow the shape of the nest.

History	Before 1803 Louisiana was the name of the whole territory drained by the river and its tributaries. Claimed for France in 1682; ceded to Spain in 1763; back again in 1800; and to the U.S.A. in 1803. Modern Louisiana became a Territory in 1804 and state on 30 April 1812. Seceded on 26 January 1861; re-admitted in July 1868
Area	52,453 sq miles
Population	4,205,900
Capital	Baton Rouge
Largest City	New Orleans
Major Products	Oil, gas, sulfur, salt, wood products, corn, livestock, sugar-cane, rice
State Motto	Union, justice and confidence
Bird	Pelican
Tree	Bald Cypress
Flower	Magnolia

MAINE

The Pine Tree State

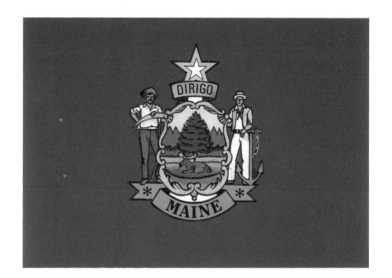

One of the chief industries of Maine is forestry which produces wood pulp and paper. In earlier times the wood was used mainly for shipbuilding and the white pine of Maine is the chief feature of the state seal of 1820. At the foot of the pine is a moose, indigenous to the state, and the supporters of the shield containing these emblems are a farmer and a sailor. These remind us that Maine is both an agricultural and a maritime state. Above the shield is a glowing North Star, indicating that Maine was then the northernmost state of the Union. The design of the arms is believed to be by Benjamin Vaughan, a native of Hallowell. The arms were used on a blue field during the Civil War, in the usual practice.

A second flag was adopted by Maine in March 1901, this time showing the pine tree in the center of a buff-colored background and with the North Star in blue within the canton. Although this is still legal it is rarely ever seen. The Civil War flag was legally adopted as the state flag on 24 February 1909 and is used with the military fringe, cord, tassels and other embellishments in the proportions of 26:33.

A third flag, a "merchant and marine" version, was adopted in July 1939. This is only for use at sea and consists of a white field on which is the pine tree with an anchor behind it. Above the tree is the state motto and below it the word "Maine," both in blue.

History	In the extreme north-east of the U.S. surrounded on three sides by Canadian territory. First settlement established in 1623. Belonged to Massachusetts from 1652 to 1820. Became a state in its own right on 15 March 1820
Area	33,265 sq miles
Population	1,124,660
Capital	Augusta
Largest City	Portland
Major Products	Potatoes, dairy products, eggs and poultry, timber and wood products, fish and seafood, paper. Tourism: about 4 million visitors annually
State Motto	*Dirigo* ("I direct")
Bird	Chickadee (1927)
Tree	White Pine (1945)
Flower	White Pine cone and tassel (1895)

MARYLAND

The Old Line State

In 1632 Sir George Calvert, who later became Lord Baltimore, was granted a royal charter by King Charles I to establish a colony north of the Potomac. The original settlers were Roman Catholics whose first township of St. Mary's was the capital until being displaced by Annapolis in 1694.

Maryland has a flag based on European heraldic tradition and comprised of elements of the arms of the Calverts and the Crosslands, Sir George's grandmother being a member of the Crossland family. The flag derives from the first state seal which on the obverse (front) showed a mounted knight in medieval Calvert-Crossland full armour. On the reverse was the quartered shield of Crossland and Calvert, together with supporters, crown, a helmet, and mottos on a scroll and around the rim. This seal was used until 1776 and revived in 1876. A different state seal had been used on a blue flag during the Civil War, following the common practice.

The Calvert arms are six vertical bands of yellow and black with a counterchanged diagonal running from the top left to the bottom right. The arms of the Crosslands are white and red quarters with a central counterchanged cross with buttons at the end of each arm. The arms of the cross had originally ended in a *fleur de lis*.

The quartered banner of the Calvert-Crosslands was taken up by the state govenor in 1901 and was officially adopted as the state flag in 1904.

History	In 1767 Mason and Dixon established its boundary with Pennsylvania on a famous line. The Proprietors ruled Maryland until 1776 when the state was formed. It ratified the U.S. Constitution on 28 April 1788
Area	10,460 sq miles
Population	4,216,975
Capital	Annapolis
Largest City	Baltimore
Major Products	Dairy products, poultry, coal, cement, electrical and electronic equipment, processed food, tourism
State Motto	*Scuto bonae voluntatis Tuae coronasti nos* ("With the shield of Thy goodwill Thou hast covered us")
Bird	Baltimore Oriole
Tree	White Oak
Flower	Black-eyed Susan

MASSACHUSETTS

The Bay State

With the distinction of having been settled by the Pilgrim Fathers, it is hardly surprising that the arms and flag of Massachusetts are among the earliest. The state was quickly involved in the Revolutionary War and in 1776 its white flag containing a pine tree and the motto "Appeal to Heaven" was soon to be widely seen.

As early as 1629 Massachusetts had a state seal, which was redesigned in 1780. An Indian from the old seal reappeared on a blue shield together with a white star to represent the United States. The shield was surmounted by a crest showing an arm holding a sword and surrounded by a scroll containing the state motto. This coat of arms appeared on the state's militia flag in 1787 and was joined in 1908 by another blue shield on the reverse side, this time containing a green pine tree. In October 1971 the reverse side was made identical to the obverse and serves as the present-day official state flag. The state governor has a triangular version of this flag with the addition of a gold fringe.

Massachusetts decided to revive its maritime flag on 1 November 1971. It is similar to the pine tree flag of 1776 but is without the "Appeal to Heaven" motto.

History	First settled by the Pilgrim Fathers in 1620; Colony formed in 1628 and played a leading part in the Revolutionary War (Maine has since been detached). Massachusetts ratified the Constitution on 6 February 1788
Area	8,284 sq miles
Population	5,737,037
Capital	Boston
Largest City	Boston
Major Products	Dairy products, poultry, fruit and vegetables, timber, fish and sea-food, electrical and electronic equipment, and machinery.
State Motto	*Ense petit placidam sub libertate quietem* ("By the sword we seek peace, but peace only under liberty")
Bird	Chickadee
Tree	American Elm
Flower	Mayflower

MICHIGAN

The Wolverine State

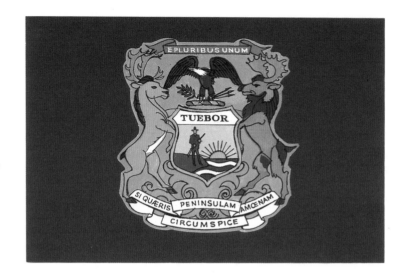

Michigan flew its first state flag in 1837, the year it achieved statehood. The flag was based on the seal of the previous Michigan Territory, that seal having in turn been based on the arms of the Hudson's Bay Company. The design of the seal was by Lewis Cass, governor of Michigan Territory, and was adopted in June 1835. The shield shows a waving figure on the shore of, presumably, Lake Michigan with the usual rising sun in the background. The supporters are an elk and a moose and between them is the crest of an American eagle similar to that on the arms of the United States. The motto above the eagle is also taken from the arms of the U.S.A., but the motto beneath the shield is a curious one. It translates as "If you are seeking a pleasant peninsula, look around you" and was possibly suggested by the inscription on a memorial tablet to the architect Sir Christopher Wren in St. Paul's Cathedral, London. That inscription reads, "Si monumentum requiris, circumspice" – "If you would see his monument look around."

The first state flag used only the seal, but later flags added the coat of arms on a blue background. The present flag has the arms on both sides and was officially adopted in 1911. The state governor's flag has a white field in place of the blue one, making the arms easier to see.

History	Michigan consists of two peninsulas between Lakes Superior, Michigan and Huron. Originally French, settled in 1668 and ceded to Britain in 1763. Part of the Indiana Territory, and conceded to the U.S.A. in 1783, became a Territory in 1805, a state on 26 January 1837
Area	58,527 sq miles
Population	9,262,078
Capital	Lansing
Largest City	Detroit
Major Products	Transport equipment, machinery, cement, chemicals, furniture, paper, maize, oats, livestock, tourism
State Motto	*Tuebor* ("I will defend")
Bird	Robin (1931)
Tree	White Pine (1955)
Flower	Apple blossom (1897)

MINNESOTA

The North Star State ◆ The Gopher State

When its seal was designed in 1858, Minnesota had replaced Maine as the most northerly state. The center of the seal presents another idealized landscape with the rising sun in the background, and an Indian rides past a farmer cultivating the prairie. The French origins of the state are emphasized in the state motto, "L'etoile du Nord."

The state militia used a flag consisting of a white field containing the seal surrounded by 18 stars plus the North Star, indicating that the state was the nineteenth to join the Union after the original 13. The reverse of the flag was plain blue. This was adopted as the state flag in April 1893, but with some slight alterations; the seal was reversed – as it had been originally – and was surrounded by flowers and ribbons. The ribbons carried the dates 1893 and 1819, the latter being the year in which Fort Snelling was established. The year of statehood appeared above the central disc with the name of the state below it. The reverse of the flag remained plain blue.

The flag was changed again in March 1957 and is now blue on both sides with the seal in color, the seal having been turned around again. The state flower, the moccasin, runs around the seal and the 19 stars and the state name are on a white disc edged in yellow. There is a movement in favor of changing the flag yet again.

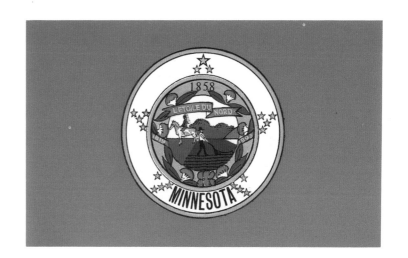

History	Explored by the French in the 1650s and claimed by France. Divided between Britain and Spain in 1763. The Spanish part became American by the Louisiana Purchase; the British part was conceded in 1783. Organized as a Territory in 1849; became a State on 11 May 1858
Area	84,402 sq miles
Population	4,075,970
Capital	St. Paul
Largest City	Minneapolis
Major Products	Iron ore and other minerals, sugarbeet, sweet corn, wheat, dairy products, mink, turkeys, cattle, wild rice, timber, machinery
State Motto	*L'etoile du Nord* ("Star of the North")
Bird	Common loon
Tree	Red Pine
Flower	Moccasin flower

MISSISSIPPI

The Magnolia State ◆ The Bayou State

Mississippi is another state where the Confederate Battle Flag can still be seen. It was incorporated into the state flag in 1894, the remainder of the flag being similar to the Stars and Bars except that the upper bar is blue instead of red (see Georgia). The Battle Flag was never mentioned by name when the specification for the Mississippi flag was drawn up, but the history of the state leaves no doubt that this was the intention. The finial of the flagstaff was clearly defined as being a spear and an axehead.

Mississippi was the second state to join the Confederacy in 1861 and during the Civil War used the Bonnie Blue Flag. This was a blue flag with one large white star and had been previously seen in West Florida when American settlers attempted to break away from Spanish rule. A second state flag in 1861 consisted of a white background containing a magnolia tree, with the Bonnie Blue Flag in the canton.

When Mississippi became a state in 1817 it adopted a coat of arms and a seal, both based on the seal of the U.S.A. The American eagle is on a blue shield but holds only six arrows rather than 13. Below the shield there are some cotton stalks and a ribbon contained the state motto. Neither the arms nor the seal were used during the time Mississippi was in secession from the Union.

History	The French set up the first settlements but ceded the area to Britain in 1763; conceded to the U.S.A. in 1783. Became a Territory in 1798, and a state in 1817. Seceded 1861; re-admitted in 1870
Area	47,689 sq miles
Population	2,520,638
Capital	Jackson
Largest City	Jackson
Major Products	Cotton, soybeans, rice, corn, timber and wood products. Tourism: about 1.5 million visits per year
State Motto	*Virtute et armis* ("By valor and arms")
Animal	White-tailed Deer (1974)
Bird	Mocking Bird (1944) Waterfowl – Wood Duck (1974)
Tree	Magnolia (1938)
Flower	Magnolia (1952)

MISSOURI

The Show Me State

The Daughters of the American Revolution were again in the forefront of a campaign to adopt a state flag for Missouri. One of the Daughters designed the flag based on the state seal on a background of the French Tricolor, to recall Missouri's history as part of the Louisiana Purchase. The design was first submitted for approval by the state legislature in 1909 but was not adopted until the third attempt on 22 March 1913. The delay was possibly caused by a feeling that all states should fly the Stars and Stripes as a symbol of unity, as has been noted earlier.

The state seal was adopted in 1822, a year after Missouri achieved statehood. It was the twenty-fourth to join the Union, as is denoted by the stars around the outer rim and in the blue sky above the arms. One half of the arms contains those of the U.S.A., the other half being divided into two quarters showing a crescent and a grizzly bear. The crescent is the old heraldic sign for a second son and in this case indicates that Missouri was the second state to be formed from the Louisiana Purchase. The two supporters are grizzly bears standing on the extremities of a scroll bearing the state motto. The date below the arms (1820) is that of the Missouri Compromise, which cleared the way for the Territory to join the Union.

History	Missouri was the "launching pad" for the Winning of the West. First settled by the French in 1735; ruled by Spain (1763-1800); sold to the U.S.A. as part of the Louisiana Purchase. Was the second Territory formed from the area (1812); became a state on 10 August 1821
Area	69,697 sq miles
Population	4,916,686
Capital	Jefferson City
Largest City	St. Louis
Major Products	Lead, zinc, coal, corn, soybeans, wheat, transport equipment
State Motto	*Salus populi suprema lex esto* ("Let the welfare of the people be the supreme law")
Bird	Bluebird (1927)
Tree	Flowering Dogwood (1955)
Flower	Hawthorn (1923)

MONTANA

The Treasure State

When troops from Montana fought in the Philippine War of 1898 they carried a flag based on the old tradition of the state seal on a blue background, but with the addition of various inscriptions. This was adopted as the state flag in February 1905, but with the inscriptions removed.

Montana became a Territory in 1864 and the seal was first seen in the following year. It consisted of a landscape showing the Rocky Mountains with the Great Falls of the Missouri River in the background. Various animals were to be seen in the original version but have since been removed. Extensive irrigation in Montana has made it a rich agricultural state, as indicated by the plough in the foreground, and the mining implements remind us that the state is also abundant in minerals. The motto refers not only to those minerals but also to the district's period under Spanish rule.

No colors were officially laid down for the seal and this was remedied in October 1981 by the specification of colors in the Pantone Matching System as used in the printing industry. At the same time the flag was changed from military dimensions to the more usual ones and "Montana" was placed above the seal.

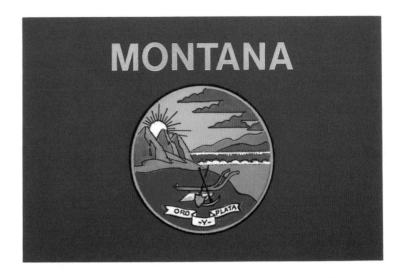

History	Montana lies mostly on the eastern side of the Rocky Mountains which give it its name. Became part of the U.S.A. with the Louisiana Purchase; sparsely settled until the gold strikes of the 1860s. Became a Territory in 1864 and a State on 8 November 1889
Area	147,138 sq miles
Population	786,690
Capital	Helena
Largest City	Billings
Major Products	Oil, copper and other minerals, wheat, tourism
State Motto	*Oro y plata* ("Gold and silver")
Bird	Western Meadowlark
Tree	Ponderosa Pine
Flower	Bitter-root

NEBRASKA

The Cornhusker State

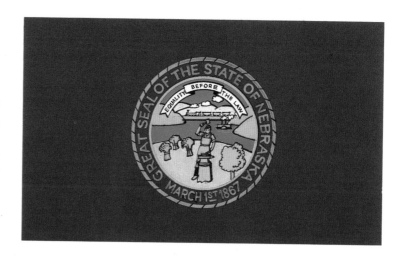

Another allegorical landscape appears on the seal of Nebraska. The state is rich in prairies with very high fertility and the crops of maize, wheat, barley and so on are reflected in the sheaves on the left. In the background a train runs along the foothills of the Rocky Mountains and a boat sails on the Missouri River. The seal was designed in 1867 by Isaac Wiles, a member of the House of Representatives. The state motto is on a scroll at the top of the seal and the date of entry to the Union appears on the rim at the bottom.

In accordance with common practice, the seal was used on flags sent to American soldiers serving in Europe during the First World War. The Daughters of the American Revolution pressed for the flag to be officially adopted, with the addition of the state flower in the canton, but they had no success until April 1925. The state legislature then gave their approval to the flag, but without the flower. It was first hoisted before a football match at the University of Nebraska in 1925 but was not officially adopted by the legislature until 1963.

During the campaign by the Daughters they had wanted to make some alterations to the seal, but the one in use is the same as the original design of 1867.

History	Nebraska is one of the leading agricultural states. First explored by Coronado in 1541 and later became part of French Louisiana. Then sold to the U.S.A. (1803); began to be settled (1847); in 1854 it became a Territory. Admitted to the Union on 1 March 1867
Area	77,355 sq miles
Population	1,569,825
Capital	Lincoln
Largest City	Omaha
Major Products	Maize, wheat, sorghum, cattle, oil
State Motto	Equality before the law
Bird	Western Meadowlark (1929)
Tree	American Elm
Flower	Goldenrod (1895)

NEVADA

The Silver State

Although Nevada also has an allegorical landscape on its state seal, it does not appear on the state flag, which is pleasingly simple in its design. It results from a competition won by Louis Shellback, although his winning design did not contain the name of the state, which was added around the white star before the flag was officially adopted on 26 March 1929. Nevada became a state during the Civil War and this is reflected in the motto. The design is completed by two sprigs of sagebrush, the state flower.

A previous flag, adopted on 22 March 1915, did use the state seal in the form of an extremely ornate shield. The name of the state appeared in white above the shield and the state motto in yellow below it. It was surrounded by 36 stars in two arcs of eighteen, the upper arc being yellow and the lower arc in white. The 36 stars indicated that Nevada was thirty-sixth in joining the Union. During its fourteen years of existence this flag was not much used, although the battleship *Nevada* received one as a gift.

An even earlier flag, adopted in February 1905, had the name of the state in the center, 36 stars in yellow and white, two large white stars and the words "Gold" and "Silver" in those colors. Gold was discovered in 1859, and in the same year a branch of the U.S. mint was established at Carson City following the discovery of the Comstock Lode, one of the richest-ever silver deposits.

History	Originally part of Mexico Nevada was ceded to the U.S.A. in 1848 and was at first attached to Utah. Gold was found in 1859, and in 1861 it became a Territory. Joined the Union on 31 October 1864
Area	110,561 sq miles
Population	800,493
Capital	Carson City
Largest City	Las Vegas
Major Products	Gold, oil, silver, cattle, hay, potatoes
State Motto	All for our country
Animal	Bighorn sheep (1973)
Bird	Mountain Bluebird
Tree	Single-leaf Piñon (1959)
Flower	Sagebrush (1959)

NEW HAMPSHIRE

The Granite State

New Hampshire was one of the original states of the Union and the first to declare its independence of Great Britain on 15 June 1776. The state seal has the optimistic rising sun in the background with a ship, supposedly the *Raleigh*, in the shipbuilding yard at Portsmouth. The *Raleigh* was one of the earliest ships of the U.S. Navy and was first launched in 1776. This seal was adopted in 1784 and used on a blue background as a military flag from 1792.

In February 1909 it was adopted as the state flag with the addition of nine stars within a laurel wreath. In 1931 the seal was redrawn and used on the flag from 1 January 1932. 1784, the date at the foot of the original seal, was replaced by 1776, the year of the state's independence declaration. In 1944 there was a move to redesign the flag completely but it came to nothing.

Perhaps as a result of this, a state emblem was adopted on 3 May 1945. It is oval in shape and contains a depiction of a rock formation called "The Old Man of the Mountains." Around the rim are the words "State of New Hampshire" together with the current state motto. The original motto was *Vis unita fortior* ("United strength is greater") and was used on a state seal of 1775 but dropped from both the 1784 and 1931 versions.

History	The state lies between Massachusetts Bay and Canada. Inland are the granite-based mountains that give it its nickname. Area was first settled in 1623 at Rye; became a separate province in 1679. An independent state government was set up in 1776, and the state ratified the U.S. Constitution on 21 June 1787
Area	9,279 sq miles
Population	920,610
Capital	Concord
Largest City	Manchester
Major Products	Hay, vegetables, apples, livestock, machinery, metalware, stone
State Motto	Live free or die
Bird	Purple Finch
Tree	White Birch
Flower	Purple Lilac

NEW JERSEY

The Garden State

Another of the original 13 states, New Jersey accompanied the others in disposing of all signs of British royal dominance in 1776. Eugene de Simitière designed a seal made up of a coat of arms. A blue shield containing three ploughs indicates the importance of agriculture to the state economy. The crest is an armored helmet topped by a horse's head and the supporters are Liberty on the left and Ceres, the Roman goddess of agriculture. These basic features were specified by the supervizing committee with the artist providing embellishments such as the date on the scroll, which was originally in the Roman numerals MDCCLXXVI.

The details and the colors to be used were not officially regulated until 1928, when the ribbon scroll was added and the date changed to Arabic figures. The arms were placed on a buff background in March 1898 to serve as a flag for the state governor, also the commander-in-chief of the state militia. The buff color came from a previous flag which had been used by troops from February 1780, with the buff the same as the facings on the soldiers' uniforms (see also Delaware). The Dutch had been the first settlers in the area around 1620 and for some time it was mistakenly thought that the buff color was derived from the Dutch Royal House of Orange. By the 1930's the flag was in general use by the public and the usage was legalized in 1938.

History	Has strong industrial activity and extensive agricultural base. First settled by the Dutch in 1623. Became an English colony in 1664, and a royal province in 1702. Independent government was set up in 1776 and the state ratified the Constitution on 18 December 1787
Area	7,787 sq miles
Population	7,364,823
Capital	Trenton
Largest City	Newark
Major Products	Chemicals, electronic and electrical equipment, machinery, tomatoes, corn, fruit
State Motto	Liberty and prosperity
Bird	Eastern Goldfinch (1935)
Tree	Red Oak
Flower	Purple Violet

NEW MEXICO

The Land of Enchantment

The very modern-looking flag of New Mexico in fact dates from 1925. It was designed by an archaeologist, Dr Harry Mera, and the Daughters of the American Revolution were yet again instrumental in its adoption on 15 March of that year. The colors of red and yellow recognize Spanish rule in the seventeenth century and Dr. Mera's archaeological knowledge led him to use the sun symbol of the Zia Indians. This symbol is described in the New Mexican flag pledge as "the Zia symbol of perfect friendship among united cultures" and also served as the basis for the layout of the state Capitol.

The flag in use before this one was light blue and had the words "New Mexico" and the Stars and Stripes in the canton. The lower fly carried the state seal and the upper fly had the number 47, signifying that New Mexico was forty-seventh to join the Union. The state seal dates from February 1887 and was readopted in March 1913, the year after New Mexico became a state. It uses the Mexican and American eagles, commemorating the sale of New Mexico to the U.S.A. in 1848.

History	The state lies around the headwaters of the Rio Grande. Name was originally applied to all the northern part of Mexico which was lost to the U.S.A. in 1848. Became a Territory in its own right in 1850, although Utah and Arizona were later separated off, other areas were lost to Texas and Colorado. Became the forty-seventh state in 1912
Area	121,335 sq miles
Population	1,302,894
Capital	Santa Fé
Largest City	Albuquerque
Major Products	Uranium and other minerals, oil, gas, cereals, cotton, livestock
State Motto	*Crescit eundo* ("It grows as it goes")
Bird	Roadrunner
Tree	Piñon
Flower	Yucca flower

NEW YORK

The Empire State

New York adopted its first constitution in 1777 and in the same year the state arms were designed, first appearing on the flag in 1778. The figures of Liberty and Justice support a shield in which boats are overlooked by the rising sun. The crest is composed of an American eagle perched on top of a globe and the state motto appears in the center of a scroll below the shield.

During the War of Revolution the military flag consisted of the arms on a blue field and in 1858 a similar flag was adopted for the state troops, but with a white background. This was changed to a buff color in April 1898, the color matching that of the soldiers' uniforms. Three years later the color reverted to blue and remains unchanged.

The state governor has a similar flag but as commander-in-chief of the state troops his flag carries a white star in each corner. His chief-of-staff has the rank of a major-general and is therefore entitled to two stars, one on each side of the crest. The chief-of-staff is normally the adjutant-general and the background color of his flag depends upon which branch of the services he comes from. The flag of an Army officer has a red background, the Air Force has light blue and dark blue is used for the Navy.

History	Henry Hudson (after whom its chief river is named) claimed the area for the Dutch in 1609. The first colonists arrived in 1624. In 1644 the colony was taken over by Britain. Independence was declared on 20 April 1777, and the state ratified the Constitution on 26 July 1788
Area	49,108 sq miles
Population	17,558,072
Capital	Albany
Largest City	New York City
Major Products	Dairy products, maize, wheat, fruit, maple syrup, titanium and other minerals, clothing, machinery, processed foods
State Motto	*Excelsior* ("Ever higher")
Bird	Bluebird
Tree	Sugar Maple
Flower	Rose

NORTH CAROLINA

The Tar Heel State ◆ The Old North State

The first English settlement of North Carolina was on Roanoke Island in 1585 but was quickly wiped out. A further settlement in 1653 survived until independence was declared in 1776, but the state did not produce a flag until secession from the Union on 20 May 1861. A resolution passed on the same day called for the creation of a flag which was adopted one month later, on 22 June. The first design had a wide vertical stripe of red and an upper horizontal bar of blue. On the red vertical was a white star with the dates of 20 May 1775 and 20 May 1861. The first date is supposedly that of the original declaration of independence and the second is the date of secession.

The flag was revised in March 1885 when the blue and red were transposed and the vertical stripe was made narrower. The white star appeared between the letters NC and the 1861 date was replaced by that on which state representatives were authorized to vote for independence.

The seal of North Carolina essentially dates from 1776 but does not appear on any flag used by the state. It shows the figures of Prosperity and Liberty, accompanied by the state motto.

History	First English permanent settlement was in 1653. The Colony of North Carolina created in 1712; declared its independence in 1776. Ratified the Constitution on 21 November 1789; seceded on 20 May 1861. Was re-admitted to the Union in 1868
Area	52,669 sq miles
Population	5,881,766
Capital	Raleigh
Largest City	Charlotte
Major Products	Tobacco, maize, soybeans, textiles, furniture, mica, minerals, timber
State Motto	*Esse quam videri* ("To be rather than to seem")
Animal	Gray Squirrel (1969)
Bird	Cardinal (1943)
Tree	Pine (1963)
Flower	Dogwood (1941)

NORTH DAKOTA

The Flickertail State

The flag seen in North Dakota today was carried by infantrymen from the state during the Philippine Campaign of 1898-99. Major John Fraine, commander of the First Battalion, later lobbied for the Color to be adopted as the state flag and legislation to confirm this was adopted on 3 March 1911. However, the original drafting of the legislation did not describe the Color correctly and it was not until 1943 that revised legislation put the matter right.

On 15 March 1957 a new flag was adopted for the National Guard since the state flag was in effect a military Color. The Guard was given a coat of arms consisting of a yellow shield in the shape of a Sioux Indian arrowhead, with a green diagonal band containing three stars and a *fleur de lis*. The motto "Strength from the soil" appears on a scroll below the shield and the crest is a bow with three arrows. These arms are on a green flag and the Governor's flag is similar but with the four stars of a commander-in-chief, one in each corner.

The state flag has thirteen stars representing the original states of the Union and an eagle flourishes a scroll bearing the national motto.

The state seal dates from 1889 and consists of an idealized landscape together with the bow and three arrows which appear on the flag of the National Guard. 42 stars represent the number of states in the Union at the time of North Dakota's admittance.

38

History	The Dakota Territory was part of the Louisiana Purchase in 1803, with the Red River valley ceded by Britain in 1818. First settled in 1819, became a Territory in 1861; in 1889 was divided into two states. North Dakota admitted to the Union on 2 November 1889
Area	70,665 sq miles
Population	652,717
Capital	Bismarck
Largest City	Fargo
Major Products	Barley, sunflowers, flaxseed, durum, wheat, oil, gas, cattle
State Motto	Liberty and union, now and forever, one and inseparable
Bird	Western Meadowlark
Tree	American Elm
Flower	Wild Prairie Rose

OHIO

The Buckeye State

The only state not to have a rectangular flag is Ohio, which adopted the pennon-shaped flag on 9 May 1902. It is based on the pennon used by the cavalry between 1862 and 1865 and was designed by John Eisenmann in 1901. The nickname of the state was being used long before the buckeye was confirmed as the state tree in 1953 and Eisenmann's design was based on the shape of the tree's seed, as its circular form on the flag could suggest both the tree itself and also the "O" for Ohio.

The name of the state comes from the Indian and means "beautiful river." Eisenmann himself said that his flag was meant to represent the river and roads of Ohio, although perhaps this is not immediately apparent. As in many other flags, the number of stars indicates the position held by the state in its joining the Union – in this case seventeenth.

The governor has a flag containing the state seal, which is another allegorical landscape showing the sun rising over the Scioto River and Mount Logan. The governor's flag is red and has thirteen stars around the state seal and one star in each corner, making the seventeen required.

A pennon is distinct from a pennant by ending in a swallow-tail shape, as shown here. A pennant tapers to a point.

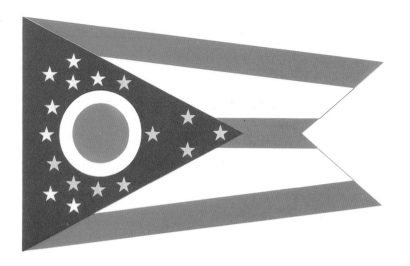

History	Settlers first arrived in area in 1788, and it was part of the Territory conceded to the U.S.A. in 1783. Was then part of the North-West Territory; became a state on 1 March 1803 (a date fixed retroactively in 1953)
Area	41,330 sq miles
Population	10,797,630
Capital	Columbus
Largest City	Cleveland
Major Products	Coal, oil, gas, maize, wheat, oats, non-electrical machinery, transport equipment
State Motto	With God all things are possible
Bird	Red Cardinal (1933)
Tree	Buckeye (1953)
Flower	Scarlet Carnation (1904)

OKLAHOMA

The Sooner State

The name of the state derives from an Indian word meaning "red people" and it is therefore fitting that Indian symbols should feature prominently in the state flag. The Daughters of the American Revolution were again instrumental in its adoption by organizing a design competition which was won by Mrs. Luise Fluke with help from Dr. Joseph Thoburn of the Oklahoma Historical Society. An olive branch and a peace pipe are crossed on an Osage shield. The light blue field and the peace pipe were derived from a flag used by the Choctaw Indians. The flag was adopted on 2 April 1925 and the name of the state was added in May 1941.

The state seal dates from 1907, the year of statehood, and was based on a design prepared for the proposed state of Sequoyah. It consists of a large white star on a blue background together with 45 smaller stars. The seal of the former Oklahoma Territory is in the center of the large star and the branches of the star contain emblems of the five Indian nations. The Territorial seal shows the figure of Liberty accompanied by an Indian and a farmer together with the present state motto.

An earlier state flag was adopted on 2 March 1911 and consisted of the number 46 within a large white star with blue edges. The star was on a red field, which became unpopular after the Russian Revolution of 1917 and led to the adoption of the new flag in 1925.

OKLAHOMA

History	One of the Great Plains states. Originally part of the Louisiana Purchase, left unorganized as the Indian Territory for many years. After opening up by white settlers it became a regular Territory in 1890; was admitted as a State on 16 November 1907
Area	69,919 sq miles
Population	3,025,290
Capital	Oklahoma City
Largest City	Oklahoma City
Major Products	Oil, gas, wheat, timber
State Motto	*Labor omnia vincit* ("Work conquers all")
State Colors	Green and white
Bird	Scissor-tailed Flycatcher
Tree	Redbud
Flower	Mistletoe

OREGON

The Beaver State

Oregon has the distinction of being the only state to retain a double-sided flag with different images on each side. The central part of the state seal appears on the obverse, consisting of a heart-shaped shield surrounded by 33 stars, the number of states in the Union when Oregon was admitted. Within the shield is an allegorical landscape depicting a wagon train arriving at the Pacific Ocean, with the rising sun in the background. The state motto appears on a scroll and below it is a wheatsheaf flanked by agricultural implements. The name and date are above and below the seal.

The reverse of the flag shows a beaver standing on its dam and is a reminder of the early fur-trapping days. Both designs are in yellow on a blue field and the flag was adopted in 1925 when it was needed to fly alongside other state flags outside the Washington Post Office building. Originally only two flags were made, but its popularity led to a law of 1953 which required it to be flown in all state schools and public buildings.

The state seal was originally designed in 1859, when Oregon achieved statehood, and the present design as used on the flag was adopted in 1903.

History	The name originally included all the territory that now includes Washington and Idaho, and was once ruled jointly by the U.S.A. and Britain (1818-48). In 1848 it became a Territory in its own right; admitted to the Union on 14 February 1859
Area	97,073 sq miles
Population	2,632,105
Capital	Salem
Largest City	Portland
Major Products	Gold and other minerals, cattle, hay, wheat, timber and wood products. Tourism: about 16 million visitors annually
State Motto	The Union
Bird	Western Meadowlark
Tree	Douglas Fir
Flower	Oregon Grape

PENNSYLVANIA

The Keystone State

The state seal of Pennsylvania was created in 1777 and officially adopted in 1791. It consists of a shield divided into three sections showing a ship, a plough and three sheaves of wheat. The crest is a standing American eagle. There is a reverse side to the seal, making it unusual as most state seals have only an obverse.

The seal appears on the state flag together with supporters consisting of two horses and the state motto is on a scroll below some sprigs of laurel. These arms were officially adopted in 1809 and were used on a blue background as the flag for the state militia. It was officially adopted as the state flag on 13 June 1907 and the present form was specified in 1964. The specification made the horses black, although they do not show up too well on a dark blue field. The state governor's flag consists of the same arms on a white background.

History	Settled in 1682 by Quakers led by William Penn. In the French and Indian War the western part of Pennsylvania was acquired, and Pittsburgh founded. Independent government established in September 1776; the state ratified the Constitution on 12 December 1787
Area	45,308 sq miles
Population	11,863,895
Capital	Harrisburg
Largest City	Philadelphia ("The City of Brotherly Love")
Major Products	Coal, iron, steel, mushrooms, tobacco, wheat and other cereals
State Motto	Virtue, liberty and independence
Animal	Whitetail Deer (1959)
Bird	Ruffed Grouse (1931)
Tree	Hemlock (1931)
Flower	Mountain Laurel (1933)

RHODE ISLAND

The Little Rhody State

The smallest of the states in the Union was founded in 1636 by Roger Williams after he had been exiled from the Massachusetts Bay Colony for religious dissent. The first state seal appeared in 1664, comprising an anchor and the word "Hope," a word which is always represented in heraldry by the anchor. During the War of the Revolution these symbols appeared on the flag of the 2nd Rhode Island Regiment, with the 13 stars of the original states in the canton. The anchor and motto were used on a blue field during the Civil War, in accordance with common practice, and in 1881 the anchor on a blue background was adopted as the official state arms.

A state flag had been in official use since March 1877 and consisted of a white field containing a blue anchor with a red outline and surrounded by a circle of 38 stars. A second design of 1 February 1882 had a yellow anchor in a red outline and a circle of 13 yellow stars, all on a blue field. The anchor had a rope wrapped around it, but this was taken away in a revised version of 1892 and five years later the current flag was officially adopted.

The state governor's flag was authorized in May 1931 and has the state arms in the center of a white field with four blue stars of a commander-in-chief, one star in each corner. The arms consist of a blue shield containing the anchor with the name of the state and the motto on scrolls above and below it.

History	The smallest state of the Union. Settlers came from Massachusetts in search of religious freedom in 1636; obtained a charter in 1663 as the Colony of Rhode Island and Providence Plantations. The state renounced allegiance to Britain on 4 May 1776 only reluctantly joined the Union on 29 May 1790
Area	1,214 sq miles
Population	947,154
Capital	Providence
Largest City	Providence
Major Products	Metalware, machinery, jewelry-silverware, transport equipment, fish
State Motto	Hope
Bird	Rhode Island Red
Tree	Maple
Flower	Violet

SOUTH CAROLINA

The Palmetto State

South Carolina is named after King Charles I of England who gave it to Robert Heath in 1629. During the War of the Revolution the cap badge of South Carolinian troops was a white crescent and this was placed on a blue background as the military flag. During the British attack on a log fort in Charleston Harbor in 1776, the palmetto wood used in the fort's construction proved so resilient that the tree was added to the flag as a tribute. This flag was adopted as the state flag of South Carolina after secession from the Union in December 1860 and remains so to this day.

In the month between secession and the adoption of this flag there were a number of other designs put forward, one of them being very similar to the Confederate Battle Flag which was recommended by the Provisional Congress on 4 March 1861. The proposed flag was red with a blue saltire charged with 15 stars, each star representing one of the "slave" states. The crescent and palmetto tree were relegated to within the canton.

However, popular feeling saw the emergence of the palmetto tree in greater prominence, particularly as it was also the badge of the state militia. It appears on the state seal which was first adopted in 1776.

History	Permanent settlements began in 1670. From 1719 the colony was a royal province. A council of safety took over in 1775 and the governor fled. Constitution ratified on 23 May 1788; seceded on 20 December 1860; re-admitted in 1868
Area	31,113 sq miles
Population	3,121,820
Capital	Columbia
Largest City	Charleston
Major Products	Tobacco, soybeans, corn, non-metallic minerals, cotton and textiles
State Motto	*Dum spiro spero* ("While I breathe I hope")/*Animas opibusque parati* ("Prepared in soul and resources")
Bird	Carolina Wren
Tree	Palmetto
Flower	Jessamine

SOUTH DAKOTA

The Sunshine State ◇ The Coyote State

The state seal which now appears on the obverse of the flag was on the reverse until 1963. From 1909 the obverse had been a large golden sun with lettering around it as on the current version and the seal appeared on the reverse in blue stitching. Commonsense and economics eventually led to their being combined and on 11 March 1963 legislation saw the seal being placed within the sun symbol with the same design on both sides of the flag.

The flag of 1909 had been designed by Senator Ernest May together with Mr. Doane Robinson, Secretary of the State Historical Society, so it was fitting that the redesign should be the work of Will Robinson who had followed his father as Secretary of the Historical Society. The band which carries the lettering around the state seal can be either white or sky-blue to match the field, as this was not particularly specified in the 1963 legislation.

The seal itself is yet another allegorical picture and mainly depicts the agricultural nature of the state. The state motto appears on a scroll at the top of the seal and the date at the foot of the surrounding band is that of statehood, which was achieved on the same day as neighbouring North Dakota.

History	Part of Dakota Territory from 1861; became a state on 2 November 1889 (the same day as North Dakota). Had been part of French Louisiana; was settled from 1857 onward, as part of Missouri Territory, especially after the Homestead Act of 1863 and the gold strike of 1874
Area	77,116 sq miles
Population	690,768
Capital	Pierre
Largest City	Sioux Falls
Major Products	Gold, silver, oats, rye, sunflower seed, processed food
State Motto	Under God the people rule
Animal	Coyote
Bird	Chinese Ringneck Pheasant
Tree	Black Hills Spruce
Flower	Pasque Flower

TENNESSEE

The Volunteer State

Some influence of the Battle Flag of the Confederacy can be seen in the flag of Tennessee which was officially adopted on 17 April 1905 and was designed by Captain LeRoy Reeves of the Third Regiment of Tennessee Infantry. The three stars symbolize the three regions of Tennessee, which are called Grand Divisions.

A previous flag was designed for the Exposition of 1897 which marked Tennessee's centenary as a member of the Union. It was made up of three diagonal red, blue and white stripes with the state nickname in gold on the blue and the figure 16 in blue on the white, again denoting entry to the Union.

President Andrew Jackson ("Old Hickory") is remembered on the state governor's flag which has a green hickory bush on a red and white wreath, all on a red background. The three stars again appear on the bush and there is one star in each corner of the flag, denoting the governor's role as commander-in-chief. The Tennessee National Guard also commemorate Andrew Jackson by having a hickory bush as their badge.

The state seal of Tennessee was adopted in 1801 but is not used on any flags.

History	First settled in 1757. The area was recognized as British in 1763. A colonial government was begun in 1772, but was annexed to North Carolina in 1776. It passed to the U.S.A. in 1790; was made a state on 1 June 1796. It seceded on 24 June 1861 and was re-admitted on 24 July 1866
Area	42,144 sq miles
Population	4,591,120
Capital	Nashville
Largest City	Memphis
Major Products	Cotton, tobacco, soybeans, wood products, iron and steel, chemicals, synthetic fibers
State Motto	Agriculture and commerce
Bird	Mocking Bird
Tree	Tulip Poplar
Flower	Iris

TEXAS

The Lone Star State

Texas was the largest state in the U.S.A. until the admission of Alaska in 1959. Its first flag appeared when it was a republic and consisted of a blue field with a large white star containing the name. In December 1836 the color of the star was changed to gold and this lasted until January 1839, when the present flag was adopted. A maritime version had the colors laid horizontally with the star in the center, and a naval ensign closely followed the Stars and Stripes until these were both abolished when Texas joined the Union in 1845. Although the origin of the single star cannot be confirmed, it is thought likely it derives from the Bonnie Blue Flag used in 1810 by the settlers in West Florida and described in the section on Mississippi.

The single star is the only emblem on the state seal and appears on a light blue disc encircled by a wreath of olive branches and oak leaves. This part of the seal is used on the state governor's flag of blue with the stars of a commander-in-chief in each corner.

The seal was adopted in 1839 and in 1961 was given a reverse side showing the coat of arms designed by a Mrs. Farnsworth and taken up by the legislature after pressure from the Daughters of the American Revolution. The shield on the arms shows the scene at the Alamo, Vince's Bridge and the Gonzales cannon, together with six flags, the Lone Star and a motto – "Texas One and Indivisible."

History	Texas is the second largest state. It was part of Mexico until 1836 when it was able to secede and form an independent republic, which was admitted to the Union on 29 December 1845. It seceded from the Union on 28 January 1861 and was re-admitted in 1870
Area	266,807 sq miles
Population	14,229,191
Capital	Austin
Largest City	Houston
Major Products	Oil, gas, cotton, maize, livestock
State Motto	Friendship
Bird	Mocking Bird (1927)
Tree	Pecan
Flower	Bluebonnet

UTAH

The Beehive State

The first Mormons (Latterday Saints) entered Salt Lake City in 1847 when it was still part of Mexico and remain the largest religious body in the state. After the area was ceded by Mexico in 1848 the Mormons founded a state which they named "Deseret," meaning honeybee. The Mormon emblem was a beehive and this was used on both the state flag and seal. The first flag was similar to the Stars and Stripes except that the canton showed an eagle holding a cannon and a beehive together with 14 white stars. In 1850 the area was declared a Territory with the new name of Utah and in 1851 the canton of the flag was changed so that the cannon no longer appeared. This flag was in use until 1860.

The state seal was adopted in 1850 and has a coat of arms consisting of a shield containing a beehive with sego lilies on either side. The lilies were eaten by the early settlers when they ran out of food and are therefore commemorated. The state motto is above the beehive and the name of the state below it. There is an American flag on either side of the shield and the crest is an eagle grasping some arrows.

After 1860 Utah had no flag until the Daughters of the American Revolution designed one with the arms of the seal in white on a blue field. This was adopted in March 1911 and changed in March 1913 to the present flag with the arms in color within a thin gold circle.

History	Utah was part of the huge area of Mexico ceded to the U.S.A. in 1848, after being settled by Mormons who founded Salt Lake City. Their state of Deseret was formed in 1849, which became Utah Territory. Mormon polygamy prevented entry to the Union, however, until 4 January 1896
Area	84,899 sq miles
Population	1,461,037
Capital	Salt Lake City
Largest City	Salt Lake City
Major Products	Copper, gold, oil, gas, barley, wheat, primary metals, fabricated metals and machinery
State Motto	Industry
Bird	Sea Gull
Tree	Blue Spruce (1933)
Flower	Sego Lily (1911)

VERMONT

The Green Mountain State

The state seal of Vermont dates from 1779 and shows a pine tree beneath which is a cow and some sheaves of wheat. It is set in a green landscape with the mountains in the background. In 1821 this became part of the state's coat of arms with a crest of a stag's head and pine branches on either side of an ornate shield. A scroll below the shield bears the state motto. During the Civil War these arms were used on a blue background and this became the state flag in June 1923.

Earlier flags included a Stars and Stripes with 17 stripes and the name of the state added to it. This first flag was adopted on 1 May 1804. A second flag was adopted on 20 October 1837, again a Stars and Stripes but with the canton containing a white star which enclosed the coat of arms.

The Bennington Battle Flag is said to have been carried by the Green Mountain Boys when Vermont declared itself independent on 16 January 1777. A replica of this flag is flown over the State House each year on the anniversary of the battle. It is an early Stars and Stripes but with the order of the stripes reversed and the number 76 within the stars. However, although it is pleasing that the early rebels are remembered in this way, the authenticity of the flag is extremely doubtful.

History	In the center of Vermont are the Green Mountains that give it its name. It was part of French Canada until 1760, after which it was disputed between New York and New Hampshire. Declared itself independent on 16 January 1777. After the Revolutionary War it was allowed to join the Union, on 4 March 1791
Area	9,614 sq miles
Population	511,456
Capital	Montpelier
Largest City	Burlington
Major Products	Dairy produce, hay, fruit, maple syrup, stone, timber, machine tools, electronics
State Motto	Freedom and unity
Bird	Hermit Thrush
Tree	Sugar Maple
Flower	Red Clover

VIRGINIA

The Old Dominion

Virginia was named in honor of Queen Elizabeth I of England and became the first permanent English settlement in North America in 1607. One of the 13 original states in the Union, Virginia took a leading part in the revolutionary struggle. The seal shows Virtus with one foot on the dead body of Tyranny, whose crown has fallen off and lies nearby. The motto translates as "Thus ever to tyrants" and recalls how Ancient Rome became the inspiration to the new states following the Revolutionary War, even down to the architectural style used in the building of state Capitols. The central seal is within a wreath and was designed in 1776 by George Wythe. There is a reverse side to the seal but this is not seen on any flag.

Virginia seceded from the Union on 17 April 1861 and the seal was in use on the flag by the end of that month, appearing on a white disc in a plain blue field. The seal was revised in 1930 and the new version first used on the flag in 1931, but the flag has remained basically unchanged since 1861. The flying end of the flag usually has a silver fringe although this is not laid down in any of the official specifications.

History	The first chartered settlement was made in Virginia in 1607 at Jamestown. Tobacco was under cultivation by 1619. In 1775 the governor had to step down and in 1781 the British surrendered at Yorktown. Virginia ratified the Constitution on 25 June 1788; seceded on 17 April 1861; was re-admitted on 26 January 1870
Area	40,767 sq miles
Population	5,346,818
Capital	Richmond
Largest City	Norfolk
Major Products	Corn, hay, peanuts, tobacco and tobacco products, coal
State Motto	Sic semper tyrannis ("Thus ever to tyrants")
Bird	Cardinal
Tree	Flowering Dogwood
Flower	Flowering Dogwood

WASHINGTON

The Evergreen State ◆ The Chinook State

Washington, the Evergreen State, appropriately uses a green flag and is the only state to do so. In the center is the state seal, created in 1889 by Charles Talcott. The members of the legislature had designed a seal based on the usual idealized landscape, but when they took their design to Talcott's store so that he could see to the cutting of it he bravely turned it down and suggested the present version. The picture of George Washington was taken from the label of a medicine bottle and the finished artwork was prepared by Grant Talcott, Charles' brother.

In 1916 the Daughters of the American Revolution wanted a flag to send to American soldiers serving in Europe and began lobbying for one to be adopted. They proposed that the state seal be centered on the green flag, but it took until 7 June 1923 for their design to be adopted. The flag has been slightly changed three times since then, the last specifications in 1967 laying down that the flag is to be dark green, with proportions of 3:5 and the diameter of the seal two-thirds of the width. The flag is sometimes seen with a gold fringe, but nothing is officially stated in the specifications.

History	The state lies in the extreme north-east and is the nearest one to Alaska; it shares the Vancouver coastline with British Columbia. It was part of the Oregon Country once shared by Britain and the U.S.A., and became a Territory in its own right in 1853 and a state on 11 November 1889
Area	68,139 sq miles
Population	4,132,156
Capital	Olympia
Largest City	Seattle
Major Products	Timber and wood products, wheat, livestock, fish, primary aluminum
State Motto	*Alki* (''By and by'')
State Color	Green and gold
Bird	Willow Goldfinch
Tree	Western Hemlock
Flower	Rhododendron

WEST VIRGINIA

The Mountain State

The western counties of Virginia formed themselves into a state in 1862 and were admitted to the Union in 1863. In the same year a state seal was adopted, the obverse of which now forms the arms to be seen on the state flag. The two figures represent agriculture and mining and they stand on either side of a rock which is inscribed with the date of admission. On a scroll within the ornate shield is the state motto. These arms first appeared on a flag in January 1864 when regimental state flags were authorized. The Louisiana Purchase Exposition of 1905 called for a flag for the state pavilion and the arms were placed on a white background with a border of red and blue, the reverse of the flag having a similar border but with a sprig of rhododendron in place of the arms. It was revised for the Jamestown Exposition two years later, when the red border was removed and a scroll was added carrying the name of the state.

The cost of producing two-sided flags led to a further revision being authorized on 7 March 1929. The rhododendron which had appeared on the reverse became a wreath on either side of the shield and the name of the state was placed on a red scroll above it.

History	West Virginia was part of Virginia until 1862. After the secession of Virginia the western counties voted to set up a new state, which was admitted to the Union by proclamation on 20 June 1863
Area	24,282 sq miles
Population	1,949,644
Capital	Charleston
Largest City	Charleston
Major Products	Coal, oil, gas, hay, corn, tobacco, livestock, primary and fabricated metal, chemicals
State Motto	Montani semper liberi ("Mountain men are always free")
Bird	Cardinal
Tree	Sugar Maple
Flower	Rhododendron

WISCONSIN

The Badger State

The arms and state seal were designed in 1851 by Governor Nelson Dewey and the Chief Justice, Edward Ryan, while they sat on the steps of a bank in New York. Wisconsin was admitted to the Union in 1848, so possibly they were both under pressure to come up with something suitable. Their design resulted in a shield with symbols in each quarter representing agriculture, mining, industry and the Great Lakes. The early prospectors lived in burrows similar to badgers' setts and are remembered in the crest of a badger beneath a scroll bearing the state motto. The supporter on the left is a sailor standing alongside a Horn of Plenty and on the right is a miner. The center of the shield has a belt containing the arms of the U.S.A. together with the national motto.

These arms appeared on the original Wisconsin flag of 25 March 1862, adopted from the flag of the state militia which had the arms on a blue background. It was a double-sided flag and had the coat of arms of the U.S.A. on the reverse. It had lapsed by 1887 but in 1913 was revived with the state arms on both sides, remaining in this form until 1980 when new legislation added the name of the state at the top and the date of admission to the Union below the coat of arms. The 1980 laws also laid down the proportions of the flag and the colors and design of the arms were specifically detailed.

History	It was first settled by the French and part of New France until 1763 when it was ceded to Britain. In 1783 Britain conceded it to the U.S.A., and it was part of the North-West Territory until 1836 when it became the Territory of Wisconsin which was admitted to the Union on 29 May 1848
Area	56,154 sq miles
Population	4,705,767
Capital	Madison
Largest City	Milwaukee
Major Products	Dairy products, mink, snap beans, hay and corn, timber and wood products, machinery, metalware, processed food, tourism
State Motto	Forward
Bird	Robin
Tree	Sugar Maple
Flower	Wood Violet

WYOMING

The Equality State

The Daughters of the American Revolution have been instrumental in the adoption of many flags and it is not surprising that the last flag in this book came into being because of their involvement. It was designed by Mrs. A.C. Keyes of Buffalo and adopted by the state legislature on 31 January 1817. Mrs. Keyes' original design showed a buffalo facing the fly of the flag, although nowadays it faces the flagstaff, and was on a blue field with a border of red and white. The colors matched those of the Stars and Stripes. The buffalo was in white and stood out in what was a simple but highly attractive design.

The seal which now appears within the shape of the buffalo was originally cut in 1893 and revised in 1921. The figure of Victory stands between two columns, around which are ribbons bearing the names of the chief products of the state such as grain and oil. The supporters are a cowboy and a miner and between their feet is the shield of the U.S.A. Wyoming was the first representative body to give women the vote, as early as 1869, and Victory holds a scroll proclaiming "Equal rights." She holds it proudly – and rightly so.

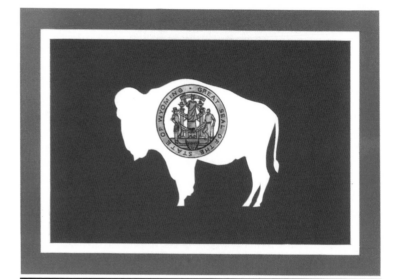

History	The eastern part was once subject to France and the western to Spain (later to Mexico). The U.S. acquired the French territory in 1803 and the Mexican in 1848. Settlers arrived from 1834 onward. A Territory was organized in 1868. It was admitted to the Union on 10 July 1890
Area	97,809 sq miles
Population	469,557
Capital	Cheyenne
Largest City	Cheyenne
Major Products	Oil, gas, coal, livestock: Tourism 5 million visitors annually
State Motto	Equal rights
Bird	Meadowlark (1927)
Tree	Cottonwood (1947)
Flower	Indian Paint Brush (1917)